Quarterly Budget/Finance Planner

Cape Turnaround™ Planner

Budget / Finance Planner (Quaterly)

Send Questions & Inquiries to info@capeturnaround.com

This Planner Belongs to:

Name: ______________________________

Address: ____________________________

____

Phone: ______________________________

E-mail: _____________________________

Quarterly Budget

INCOME

Source	Month	Month	Month

SAVINGS/INVESTMENTS

Date	Amount	Account Deposited

Date	Amount	Account Deposited

Quarter Action Plan

Bill Tracker

Bill	Amount Due	PAID			Comments
		Month	Month	Month	

Expense Tracker

Description	Category	Date Paid	Amount	Payment	Comments

Expense Tracker

Description	Category	Date Paid	Amount	Payment	Comments

Expense Tracker

Description	Category	Date Paid	Amount	Payment	Comments

Expense Tracker

Description	Category	Date Paid	Amount	Payment	Comments

Expense Tracker

Description	Category	Date Paid	Amount	Payment	Comments

Expense Tracker

Description	Category	Date Paid	Amount	Payment	Comments

Quarterly Budget Review

Summary

	Month	Month	Month
Income			
Expenses			
Savings			
Misc.			
Net Balance			

Summary of Goals Met / Budget Wins

What did not work? / Plans for Improvement

Notes

Notes

Notes

Quarterly Budget

INCOME

Source	Month	Month	Month

SAVINGS/INVESTMENTS

Date	Amount	Account Deposited

Date	Amount	Account Deposited

Quarter Action Plan

Bill Tracker

Bill	Amount Due	PAID			Comments
		Month	Month	Month	

Expense Tracker

Description	Category	Date Paid	Amount	Payment	Comments

Expense Tracker

Description	Category	Date Paid	Amount	Payment	Comments

Expense Tracker

Description	Category	Date Paid	Amount	Payment	Comments

Expense Tracker

Description	Category	Date Paid	Amount	Payment	Comments

Expense Tracker

Description	Category	Date Paid	Amount	Payment	Comments

Expense Tracker

Description	Category	Date Paid	Amount	Payment	Comments

Quarterly Budget Review

Summary

	Month	Month	Month
Income			
Expenses			
Savings			
Misc.			
Net Balance			

Summary of Goals Met / Budget Wins

What did not work? / Plans for Improvement

Notes

Notes

Notes

Quarterly Budget

INCOME

Source	Month	Month	Month

SAVINGS/INVESTMENTS

Date	Amount	Account Deposited

Date	Amount	Account Deposited

Quarter Action Plan

Bill Tracker

Bill	Amount Due	PAID			Comments
		Month	Month	Month	

Expense Tracker

Description	Category	Date Paid	Amount	Payment	Comments

Expense Tracker

Description	Category	Date Paid	Amount	Payment	Comments

Expense Tracker

Description	Category	Date Paid	Amount	Payment	Comments

Expense Tracker

Description	Category	Date Paid	Amount	Payment	Comments

Expense Tracker

Description	Category	Date Paid	Amount	Payment	Comments

Expense Tracker

Description	Category	Date Paid	Amount	Payment	Comments

Quarterly Budget Review

Summary

	Month	Month	Month
Income			
Expenses			
Savings			
Misc.			
Net Balance			

Summary of Goals Met / Budget Wins

What did not work? / Plans for Improvement

Notes

Notes

Notes

Quarterly Budget

INCOME

Source	Month	Month	Month

SAVINGS/INVESTMENTS

Date	Amount	Account Deposited

Date	Amount	Account Deposited

Quarter Action Plan

Bill Tracker

Bill	Amount Due	PAID			Comments
		Month	Month	Month	

Expense Tracker

Description	Category	Date Paid	Amount	Payment	Comments

Expense Tracker

Description	Category	Date Paid	Amount	Payment	Comments

Expense Tracker

Description	Category	Date Paid	Amount	Payment	Comments

Expense Tracker

Description	Category	Date Paid	Amount	Payment	Comments

Expense Tracker

Description	Category	Date Paid	Amount	Payment	Comments

Expense Tracker

Description	Category	Date Paid	Amount	Payment	Comments

Quarterly Budget Review

Summary

	Month	Month	Month
Income			
Expenses			
Savings			
Misc.			
Net Balance			

Summary of Goals Met / Budget Wins

What did not work? / Plans for Improvement

Notes

Notes

Notes

Quarterly Budget

INCOME

Source	Month	Month	Month

SAVINGS/INVESTMENTS

Date	Amount	Account Deposited

Date	Amount	Account Deposited

Quarter Action Plan

Bill Tracker

Bill	Amount Due	PAID			Comments
		Month	Month	Month	

Expense Tracker

Description	Category	Date Paid	Amount	Payment	Comments

Expense Tracker

Description	Category	Date Paid	Amount	Payment	Comments

Expense Tracker

Description	Category	Date Paid	Amount	Payment	Comments

Expense Tracker

Description	Category	Date Paid	Amount	Payment	Comments

Expense Tracker

Description	Category	Date Paid	Amount	Payment	Comments

Expense Tracker

Description	Category	Date Paid	Amount	Payment	Comments

Quarterly Budget Review

Summary

	Month	Month	Month
Income			
Expenses			
Savings			
Misc.			
Net Balance			

Summary of Goals Met / Budget Wins

What did not work? / Plans for Improvement

Notes

Notes

Notes

Quarterly Budget

INCOME

Source	Month	Month	Month

SAVINGS/INVESTMENTS

Date	Amount	Account Deposited

Date	Amount	Account Deposited

Quarter Action Plan

Bill Tracker

Bill	Amount Due	PAID			Comments
		Month	Month	Month	

Expense Tracker

Description	Category	Date Paid	Amount	Payment	Comments

Expense Tracker

Description	Category	Date Paid	Amount	Payment	Comments

Expense Tracker

Description	Category	Date Paid	Amount	Payment	Comments

Expense Tracker

Description	Category	Date Paid	Amount	Payment	Comments

Expense Tracker

Description	Category	Date Paid	Amount	Payment	Comments

Expense Tracker

Description	Category	Date Paid	Amount	Payment	Comments

Quarterly Budget Review

Summary

	Month	Month	Month
Income			
Expenses			
Savings			
Misc.			
Net Balance			

Summary of Goals Met / Budget Wins

What did not work? / Plans for Improvement

Notes

Notes

Notes

Quarterly Budget

INCOME

Source	Month	Month	Month

SAVINGS/INVESTMENTS

Date	Amount	Account Deposited

Date	Amount	Account Deposited

Quarter Action Plan

Bill Tracker

Bill	Amount Due	PAID			Comments
		Month	Month	Month	

Expense Tracker

Description	Category	Date Paid	Amount	Payment	Comments

Expense Tracker

Description	Category	Date Paid	Amount	Payment	Comments

Expense Tracker

Description	Category	Date Paid	Amount	Payment	Comments

Expense Tracker

Description	Category	Date Paid	Amount	Payment	Comments

Expense Tracker

Description	Category	Date Paid	Amount	Payment	Comments

Expense Tracker

Description	Category	Date Paid	Amount	Payment	Comments

Quarterly Budget Review

Summary

	Month	Month	Month
Income			
Expenses			
Savings			
Misc.			
Net Balance			

Summary of Goals Met / Budget Wins

What did not work? / Plans for Improvement

Notes

Notes

Notes

Quarterly Budget

INCOME

Source	Month	Month	Month

SAVINGS/INVESTMENTS

Date	Amount	Account Deposited

Date	Amount	Account Deposited

Quarter Action Plan

Bill Tracker

Bill	Amount Due	PAID			Comments
		Month	Month	Month	

Expense Tracker

Description	Category	Date Paid	Amount	Payment	Comments

Expense Tracker

Description	Category	Date Paid	Amount	Payment	Comments

Expense Tracker

Description	Category	Date Paid	Amount	Payment	Comments

Expense Tracker

Description	Category	Date Paid	Amount	Payment	Comments

Expense Tracker

Description	Category	Date Paid	Amount	Payment	Comments

Expense Tracker

Description	Category	Date Paid	Amount	Payment	Comments

Quarterly Budget Review

Summary

	Month	Month	Month
Income			
Expenses			
Savings			
Misc.			
Net Balance			

Summary of Goals Met / Budget Wins

What did not work? / Plans for Improvement

Notes

Notes

Notes

Savings Goals

Savings For?	
Savings Goal	
Deadline	

Savings For?	
Savings Goal	
Deadline	

Savings For?	
Savings Goal	
Deadline	

Savings For?	
Savings Goal	
Deadline	

Savings For?	
Savings Goal	
Deadline	

Savings For?	
Savings Goal	
Deadline	

Savings For?	
Savings Goal	
Deadline	

Savings For?	
Savings Goal	
Deadline	

Savings For?	
Savings Goal	
Deadline	

Savings For?	
Savings Goal	
Deadline	

Savings For?	
Savings Goal	
Deadline	

Notes

Savings Tracker

Date	Deposit/Draw	Balance	Purpose

Savings Tracker

Date	Deposit/Draw	Balance	Purpose

Savings Tracker

Date	Deposit/Draw	Balance	Purpose

Debt Tracker

Account	
Beginning Balance	
Minimum Payment Due	

Date Paid	Amount Paid	Current Balance

Account	
Beginning Balance	
Minimum Payment Due	

Date Paid	Amount Paid	Current Balance

Account	
Beginning Balance	
Minimum Payment Due	

Date Paid	Amount Paid	Current Balance

Account	
Beginning Balance	
Minimum Payment Due	

Date Paid	Amount Paid	Current Balance

Notes

Debt Tracker

Account		
Beginning Balance		
Minimum Payment Due		
Date Paid	Amount Paid	Current Balance

Account		
Beginning Balance		
Minimum Payment Due		
Date Paid	Amount Paid	Current Balance

Account		
Beginning Balance		
Minimum Payment Due		
Date Paid	Amount Paid	Current Balance

Account		
Beginning Balance		
Minimum Payment Due		
Date Paid	Amount Paid	Current Balance

Notes

Debt Tracker

Account		
Beginning Balance		
Minimum Payment Due		
Date Paid	Amount Paid	Current Balance

Account		
Beginning Balance		
Minimum Payment Due		
Date Paid	Amount Paid	Current Balance

Account		
Beginning Balance		
Minimum Payment Due		
Date Paid	Amount Paid	Current Balance

Account		
Beginning Balance		
Minimum Payment Due		
Date Paid	Amount Paid	Current Balance

Notes

Debt Tracker

Account	
Beginning Balance	
Minimum Payment Due	

Date Paid	Amount Paid	Current Balance

Account	
Beginning Balance	
Minimum Payment Due	

Date Paid	Amount Paid	Current Balance

Account	
Beginning Balance	
Minimum Payment Due	

Date Paid	Amount Paid	Current Balance

Account	
Beginning Balance	
Minimum Payment Due	

Date Paid	Amount Paid	Current Balance

Notes

Debt Tracker

Account	
Beginning Balance	
Minimum Payment Due	

Date Paid	Amount Paid	Current Balance

Account	
Beginning Balance	
Minimum Payment Due	

Date Paid	Amount Paid	Current Balance

Account	
Beginning Balance	
Minimum Payment Due	

Date Paid	Amount Paid	Current Balance

Account	
Beginning Balance	
Minimum Payment Due	

Date Paid	Amount Paid	Current Balance

Notes

Debt Tracker

Account		
Beginning Balance		
Minimum Payment Due		
Date Paid	Amount Paid	Current Balance

Account		
Beginning Balance		
Minimum Payment Due		
Date Paid	Amount Paid	Current Balance

Account		
Beginning Balance		
Minimum Payment Due		
Date Paid	Amount Paid	Current Balance

Account		
Beginning Balance		
Minimum Payment Due		
Date Paid	Amount Paid	Current Balance

Notes

Debt Tracker

Account		
Beginning Balance		
Minimum Payment Due		
Date Paid	Amount Paid	Current Balance

Account		
Beginning Balance		
Minimum Payment Due		
Date Paid	Amount Paid	Current Balance

Account		
Beginning Balance		
Minimum Payment Due		
Date Paid	Amount Paid	Current Balance

Account		
Beginning Balance		
Minimum Payment Due		
Date Paid	Amount Paid	Current Balance

Notes

Debt Tracker

Account	
Beginning Balance	
Minimum Payment Due	

Date Paid	Amount Paid	Current Balance

Account	
Beginning Balance	
Minimum Payment Due	

Date Paid	Amount Paid	Current Balance

Account	
Beginning Balance	
Minimum Payment Due	

Date Paid	Amount Paid	Current Balance

Account	
Beginning Balance	
Minimum Payment Due	

Date Paid	Amount Paid	Current Balance

Notes

Debt Tracker

Account		
Beginning Balance		
Minimum Payment Due		
Date Paid	Amount Paid	Current Balance

Account		
Beginning Balance		
Minimum Payment Due		
Date Paid	Amount Paid	Current Balance

Account		
Beginning Balance		
Minimum Payment Due		
Date Paid	Amount Paid	Current Balance

Account		
Beginning Balance		
Minimum Payment Due		
Date Paid	Amount Paid	Current Balance

Notes

Debt Tracker

Account	
Beginning Balance	
Minimum Payment Due	

Date Paid	Amount Paid	Current Balance

Account	
Beginning Balance	
Minimum Payment Due	

Date Paid	Amount Paid	Current Balance

Account	
Beginning Balance	
Minimum Payment Due	

Date Paid	Amount Paid	Current Balance

Account	
Beginning Balance	
Minimum Payment Due	

Date Paid	Amount Paid	Current Balance

Notes

Debt Tracker

Account	
Beginning Balance	
Minimum Payment Due	

Date Paid	Amount Paid	Current Balance

Account	
Beginning Balance	
Minimum Payment Due	

Date Paid	Amount Paid	Current Balance

Account	
Beginning Balance	
Minimum Payment Due	

Date Paid	Amount Paid	Current Balance

Account	
Beginning Balance	
Minimum Payment Due	

Date Paid	Amount Paid	Current Balance

Notes

Debt Tracker

Account		
Beginning Balance		
Minimum Payment Due		
Date Paid	Amount Paid	Current Balance

Account		
Beginning Balance		
Minimum Payment Due		
Date Paid	Amount Paid	Current Balance

Account		
Beginning Balance		
Minimum Payment Due		
Date Paid	Amount Paid	Current Balance

Account		
Beginning Balance		
Minimum Payment Due		
Date Paid	Amount Paid	Current Balance

Notes

Notes

Notes

Notes

Notes

Made in the USA
Monee, IL
05 November 2026

67380079R00070